blue mind mantras

blue mind
mantras

for serenity, calm,
and happiness

CICO BOOKS
LONDON NEW YORK

Published in 2021 by CICO Books
An imprint of Ryland Peters & Small Ltd
20–21 Jockey's Fields   341 E 116th St
London WC1R 4BW   New York, NY 10029

www.rylandpeters.com

10 9 8 7 6 5 4 3 2 1

A CIP catalog record for this book is available from the Library
of Congress and the British Library.

ISBN: 978-1-80065-034-3

Printed in China

Commissioning editor: Kristine Pidkameny
Senior editor: Carmel Edmonds
Senior designer: Emily Breen
Art director: Sally Powell
Production manager: Gordana Simakovic
Publishing manager: Penny Craig
Publisher: Cindy Richards

MIX
Paper from
responsible sources
FSC® C106563
www.fsc.org

introduction

The gentle splashing of waves reaching the shore... the shimmering ripples across a lake as a breeze blows over it... the scent of fresh, salty air... Water, and the elements associated with it, whether ocean, lake, or even swimming pool, can evoke an immediate sensory response in us—they calm us and soothe us. And this has been backed up by scientific research, with studies indicating that being near or in water can lower stress and anxiety, increasing overall well-being and happiness, and this mildly meditative state has been called a "blue mind" response.

Spending time in the restorative world of water and the color blue opens and transforms our awareness with natural ease. It benefits both mind and body: our senses are heightened, creativity is enhanced, and feelings of being more present in the moment emerge. We are changed for the better in bringing the power of the "blue mind" experience into our everyday; we are reminded of our connection to nature and gratitude for its gifts.

Within these pages, you'll find beautiful, evocative images, along with peaceful and inspiring mantras and quotations. From the color blue to words describing how we feel being in or around water, welcome the benefits of "blue mind" into your life.

INDIVIDUALLY, WE ARE
ONE DROP.
TOGETHER, WE ARE
AN OCEAN.

RYUNOSUKE SATORO

seeing the sea

Our need for water is about more than just staying hydrated. We're endlessly fascinated by and connected to it. As Wallace J. Nichols wrote in *Blue Mind: The Surprising Science that Shows How Being Near, In, On, or Under Water Can Make You Happier, Healthier, More Connected, and Better at What You Do* (2014), "water is changing all the time, but it's also fundamentally familiar. It seems to entertain our brains nicely with novelty plus a soothing regular background."

Numerous scientific studies support the idea that just being near a body of water is good for body and mind. For example, analysis in 2012 by the University of Exeter found that the closer people lived to the coast, the healthier they tended to be.

Another study considered how seeing water scenes or "blue" environments can affect our health. The researchers studied the physical and psychological effects of urban (gray), park/woodland (green), and river/coastline (blue) views on post-menopausal women as they rode stationary bikes for 15 minutes. The cyclists who were looking at blue scenes reported that the time seemed to go faster, and they were more willing to keep exercising.

Fortunately for the 60% of us who don't live near a coastline, even periodic visits can help us to flourish. Researchers from Kobe University in Japan affirm that humans thrive in natural environments and that visits to them can reduce stress and provide a sense of restoration. They also found that merely living near the beach isn't as helpful as stopping to take the time to appreciate the ocean view.

water meditations

You don't need to live near the ocean or even know how to swim to find healing through water. Consider adding a water meditation to your self-care practice.

A simple form of meditation which you can do with this book is to sit by your favorite body of water or even look at a glass of tap water, and contemplate any of the inspiring quotations and mantras.

Water-bowl meditation

Zen teacher Bonnie Myotai Treace of Hermitage Heart in Asheville, North Carolina, teaches a simple and beautiful water-bowl meditation. She describes it as "a way of shaping mind and heart, recognizing our intimacy with life."

- Fill a small bowl with water.

- Put it in a place that is meaningful to you—on an altar if you have one, the sill of a window with a favorite view, or even your desk.

- Top up the bowl whenever it gets low, or every day if you're not in a situation where water is scarce. Some people use snow in winter.

- Every time you fill the bowl, think about these words: *I offer this fresh water in recognition that my body and the body of all things are water. We are one thing even as we are different expressions. I vow to live this day in this wisdom, with kindness and generosity.*

I NEVER GET TIRED OF A BLUE SKY.

VINCENT VAN GOGH

IN ONE DROP OF WATER
ARE FOUND ALL THE
SECRETS OF THE OCEANS.

KAHLIL GIBRAN

Marvel at the
blue of the sea
and be happy

Only from the heart
can you touch the sky.

RUMI

PRESENT MOMENT,
PRESENT CARE

When I sit here by the sea and listen to the sound of waves, I feel free from all obligations and people of this world.

HENRY DAVID THOREAU

Water is the driving force of all nature.

LEONARDO DA VINCI

Blue thou art, intensely blue;
Flower, whence came thy
dazzling hue?

JAMES MONTGOMERY

I followed my
heart and it led me
to the beach.

ANONYMOUS

There's no better sound to hear than the ocean, the wind, and the rain all at once, late at night.

ANONYMOUS

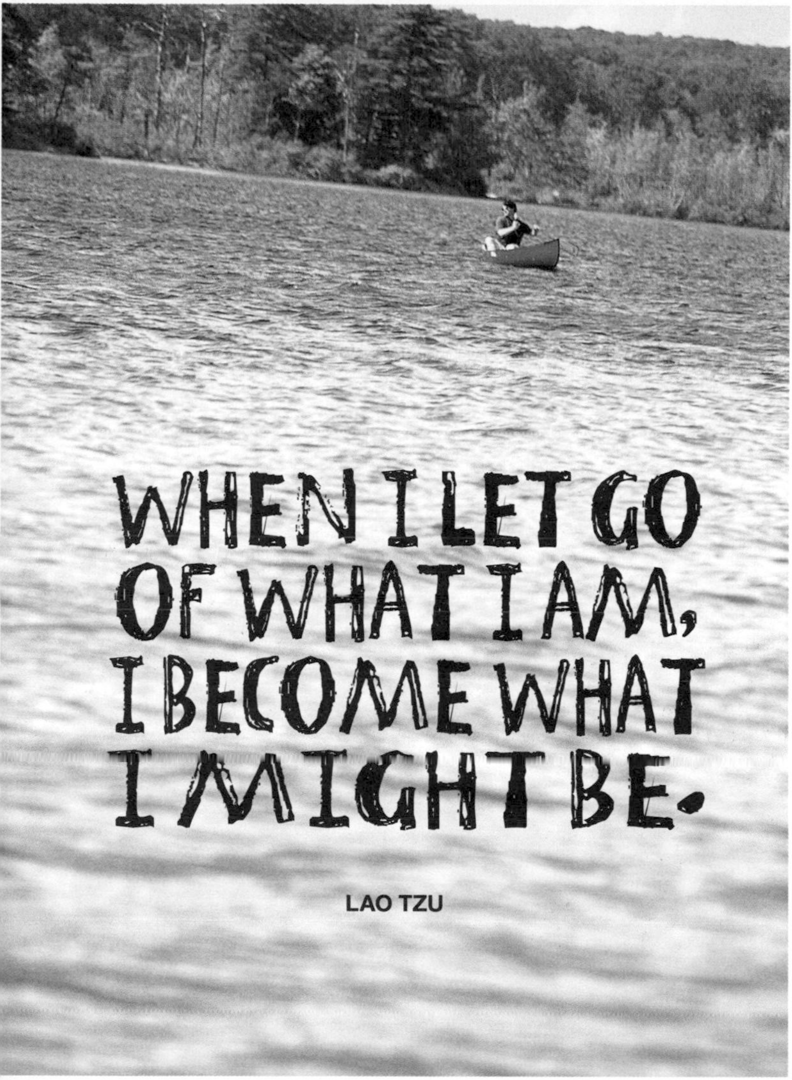

WHEN I LET GO
OF WHAT I AM,
I BECOME WHAT
I MIGHT BE.

LAO TZU

Sometimes in the winds of change,
we find our true direction.

ANONYMOUS

MY SOUL IS FULL OF LONGING FOR THE SECRET
OF THE SEA, AND THE HEART OF THE GREAT OCEAN
SENDS A THRILLING PULSE THROUGH ME.

HENRY WADSWORTH LONGFELLOW

Memories of the sea lift my
spirit and soothe my soul

THERE REALLY IS NO BETTER
TIME THAN NOW.

SIR WALTER SCOTT

Live in the sunshine, swim the sea,
drink the wild air.

RALPH WALDO EMERSON

He who hears the rippling
of rivers will not utterly
despair of anything.

HENRY DAVID THOREAU

The voice of the sea is seductive; never ceasing, whispering, clamoring, murmuring, inviting the soul to wander for a spell in abysses of solitude.

KATE CHOPIN

BLUE ON BLUE

Settle into
the tranquility
of now

PAUSE
REHYDRATE
REPEAT

MEET YOUR TRUE SELF

That blue and bright-eyed floweret of the brook,
Hope's gentle gem, the sweet Forget-me-not!

SAMUEL TAYLOR COLERIDGE

Above the clouds, the sky is always blue.

THÉRÈSE OF LISIEUX

The open Sky sits upon our senses like a Sapphire Crown—the Air is our robe of state—the Earth is our throne, and the Sea a mighty Minstrell playing before it …

JOHN KEATS

THE WATERFALL WINKS AT EVERY PASSERBY.

UNKNOWN

We dream in colors
borrowed from the sea.

UNKNOWN

When you do things from your soul,
you feel a river moving in you, a joy.

RUMI

MY GUIDING
WORD IS
SERENITY

THE SEA! The sea! The open sea!
The blue, the fresh, the ever free!

BRYAN PROCTER

Truth lifts the heart,
like water refreshes thirst.

RUMI

Still waters run deep.

ENGLISH PROVERB

Everything turns on your assumptions about it, and that's on you. You can pluck out the hasty judgment at will, and like steering a ship around the point, you will find calm seas, fair weather, and a safe port.

MARCUS AURELIUS

BLUE OPENS THE WAY
TO INNER PEACE

I'm not afraid of storms, for I'm learning how to sail my ship.

LOUISA MAY ALCOTT

Blue is a soft place to land

Music in the soul
can be heard by
the universe.

LAO TZU

Catch the magic

Never give up, for that is just the place and time the tide will turn.

HARRIET BEECHER STOWE

There is always
something to be
grateful for

Relax to the sound of the gentle evening rain

LIFE IS LIKE THE OCEAN—
AN OPEN INVITATION

I know the joy of fishes in the river through my
own joy, as I go walking along the same river

CHUANG TZU

Make your heart like a lake,
with a calm, still surface,
and great depths of kindness.

LAO TZU

GREEN CALM BELOW, BLUE QUIETNESS ABOVE.

JOHN GREENLEAF WHITTIER

Blue color is everlastingly appointed by
the deity to be a source of delight.

JOHN RUSKIN

NEVER STOP
LOOKING UP

Who could be so lucky?
Who comes to a lake
for water and sees the
reflection of moon.

RUMI

LOVE IS THE RIVER OF LIFE IN THE WORLD.

HENRY WARD BEECHER

AS THE SKY
DARKENS,
WE REST

In the sky, there is no distinction of east and west; people create distinctions out of their own minds and then believe them to be true.

BUDDHA

You could not step twice into the same rivers; for other waters are ever flowing on to you.

HERACLITUS

I CONNECT WITH
MY TRUE SELF

I will do water—beautiful blue water.

CLAUDE MONET

You don't have to travel around the world to understand that the sky is blue everywhere.

JOHANN WOLFGANG VON GOETHE

WHEREVER YOU GO, GO WITH ALL YOUR HEART.

CONFUCIUS

The little windflower, whose just opened
eye is blue as the spring heaven it gazes at.

WILLIAM CULLEN BRYANT

The greatest miracle of
all is found in what is
most ordinary

We cannot see our reflection in running water. It is only in still water that we can see.

ZEN SAYING

Nothing is softer or more
flexible than water,
yet nothing can resist it.

LAO TZU

OPEN YOUR EYES AND SEE THE
BEAUTY THAT SURROUNDS YOU

You will always find
an answer in the sound
of water.

ZHUANGZI

QUIET
YOUR
MIND

Raise your words,
not your voice.
It is rain that grows
flowers, not thunder.

RUMI

Adopt the pace
of nature.

RALPH WALDO EMERSON

LIFE IS HAPPENING RIGHT NOW

Listen to water

Imagine flying into the blue

Water expands our horizons and
nourishes our perspective

WATER SUSTAINS
EVERYTHING

Where the waters do agree,
it is quite wonderful
the relief they give.

JANE AUSTEN

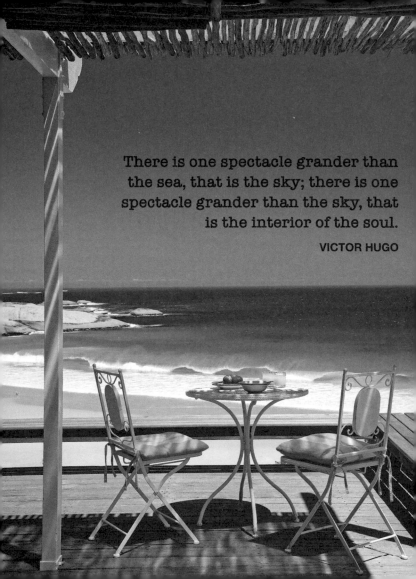

There is one spectacle grander than
the sea, that is the sky; there is one
spectacle grander than the sky, that
is the interior of the soul.

VICTOR HUGO

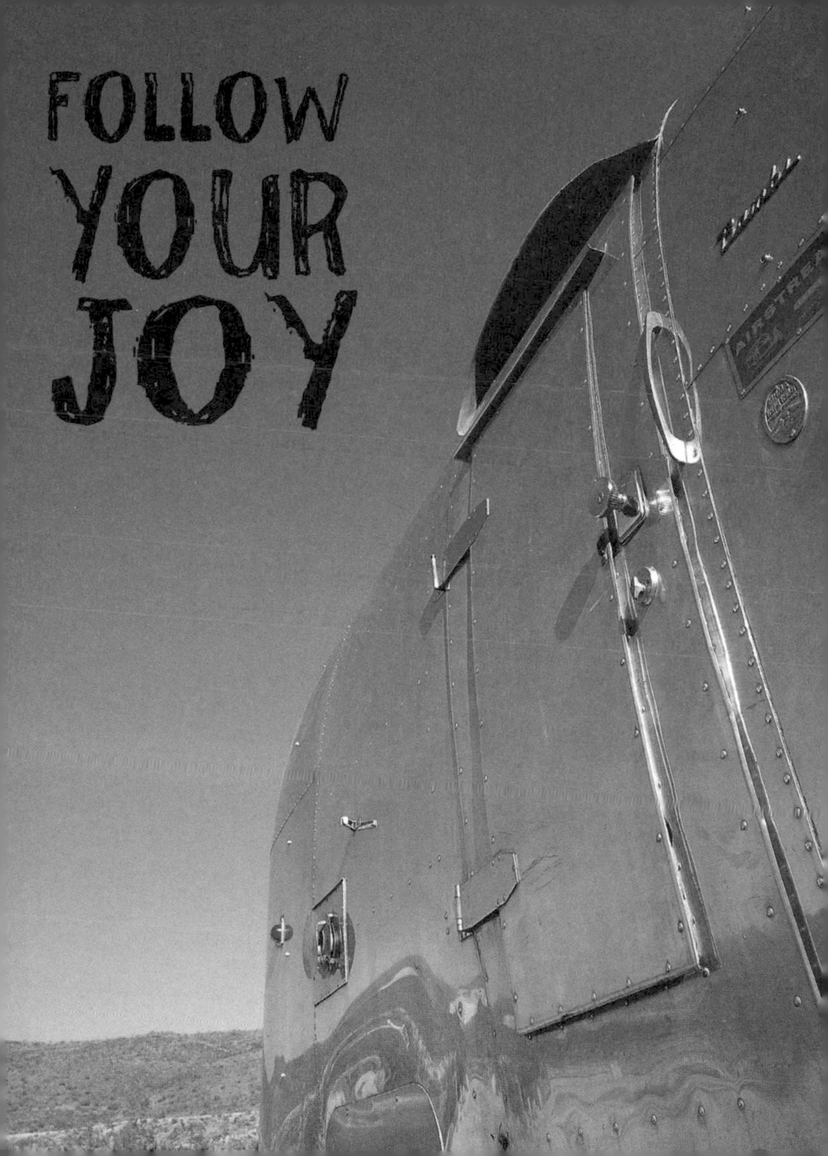
FOLLOW
YOUR
JOY

I BELIEVE THAT IF ONE ALWAYS LOOKED AT THE SKIES, ONE WOULD END UP WITH WINGS.

GUSTAVE FLAUBERT

The Tree that is beside
the running water is fresher
and gives more fruit.

SAINT TERESA OF ÁVILA

Let the waters settle and you will see the moon and the stars mirrored in your own being.

RUMI

Happiness is a long soak
and quiet time to relax

WONDER IS THE BEGINNING
OF WISDOM.

SOCRATES

The simple joys
are the great ones

Happiness not in another place but this place... not for another hour, but this hour.

WALT WHITMAN

Each day provides its own gifts.

MARCUS AURELIUS

Oh, the summer night,
Has a smile of light,
And she sits on a
sapphire throne.

BYRAN PROCTER

Now and then it's good to pause in our pursuit of happiness and just be happy.

GUILLAUME APOLLINAIRE

The sky is the daily
bread of the eyes.

RALPH WALDO EMERSON

The real voyage of discovery consists not in seeking new landscapes, but in having new eyes.

MARCEL PROUST

AWAKENED AWARENESS
IS YOUR TRUE NATURE

PEACE
OF MIND

BE CALM TODAY

Roll on, thou deep and dark blue ocean.

LORD BYRON

If you want to
be happy, be.

LEO TOLSTOY

The pursuit, even of the best things, ought to be calm and tranquil.

MARCUS TULLIUS CICERO

To the mind that is still,
the whole universe surrenders.

LAO TZU

Make space for
your dreams

The voice
of the sea
speaks to
the soul.

KATE CHOPIN

WE DO NOT LEARN FROM
EXPERIENCE... WE LEARN
FROM REFLECTING ON
EXPERIENCE

Connect with your
divine source

Follow the river and you
will find the sea.

FRENCH PROVERB

WATER
UNITES

Take time for you:
imagine the possibilities

In rivers, the water that you touch
is the last of what has passed and
the first of that which comes;
so with present time.

LEONARDO DA VINCI

SYNCHRONIZE WITH NATURE

Breathe in
Breathe out
Get quiet

Be happy for this moment.
This moment is your life.

OMAR KHAYYAM

Worrying will never change the outcome: let it go.

DOWNTIME IS YOUR TIME

Drink deeply.
Live in serenity and joy.

BUDDHA

The touch of the sea is sensuous,
enfolding the body in its soft,
close embrace.

KATE CHOPIN

A LITTLE SEA-BATHING WOULD
SET ME UP FOREVER.

JANE AUSTEN

Returning to the source
is serenity.

LAO TZU

Tomorrow is a new day.
You shall begin it well and serenely.

RALPH WALDO EMERSON

picture credits

Jan Baldwin: pp. 20, 21, 38, 60, 63, 64, 82, 102, 105, 128, 135, 142

Martin Brigdale: p. 62

Simon Brown: p. 104

Earl Carter: pp. 2, 13, 16, 35, 44, 51, 55, 69, 89, 98, 103, 108, 110, 118, 119, 122, 134, 137, 140

Peter Cassidy: pp. 12, 65, 126

Christopher Drake: pp. 1, 27, 123

Melanie Eclare: p. 114

Chris Everard: p. 01, 95

Georgia Glynn-Smith: p. 18

Gavin Kingcome: p. 79

Mark Lohman: p. 132

Paul Massey: pp. 19, 22, 30, 32, 47, 58, 72, 78, 83, 88, 91, 111, 112

David Merewether: p. 70

James Merrell: p. 141

Emma Mitchell: p. 133

Claire Richardson: p. 136

Paul Ryan: p. 17

Mark Scott: pp. 9, 15, 25, 28, 42, 45, 46, 48, 50, 53, 56, 66, 68, 75, 84, 85, 87, 94, 96, 100, 124, 138

Lucinda Symons: pp. 10, 43

Debi Treloar: pp. 26, 33, 39, 52, 99, 115

Chris Tubbs: pp. 6, 41, 57, 67, 74, 80, 90, 92, 97, 107, 116, 120, 125, 131

Ian Wallace: pp. 5, 14, 24, 71, 106, 117, 127

Kate Whitaker: p. 34

Rachel Whiting: p. 130

Alan Williams: p. 77

Francesca Yorke: p. 59

© Soeren Schulz/
Shutterstock.com: p. 37

© PHOTO JUNCTION/
Shutterstock.com: p. 76

references

Wallace J. Nichols, *Blue Mind* (Little, Brown 2014), p. 155

Benedict W. Wheeler et al., "Does Living by the Coast Improve Health and Wellbeing?," *Health & Place*, 18/5 (September 2012), pp. 1198–1201, www.doi.org/10.1016/j.healthplace.2012.06.015.

Mathew P. White et al., "The Effects of Exercising in Different Natural Environments on Psycho-Physiological Outcomes in Post-Menopausal Women: A Simulation Study," *International Journal of Environmental Research and Public Health*, 12 (2015), pp. 11, 929–53, www.doi.org/10.3390/ijerph120911929